6ᵗʰ Gr   1991-92   OPRC

(OULD YOU EVER?

Fly to the Stars

By Dr. David Darling

DILLON PRESS, INC.
Minneapolis, Minnesota 55415

Library of Congress Cataloging-in-Publication Data

Darling, David J.
    Could you ever fly to the stars? /
    David Darling.
        p.   cm.

    Summary: Describes present-day rockets and spacecraft, explaining the limits on their speed and uses in space exploration, proposed interstellar spacecraft, and which stars would be likely destinations of future travel.
    ISBN 0-87518-446-4 (lib. bdg.) : $14.95
    1. Interstellar travel—Juvenile literature. [1. Interstellar travel.   2. Space flight.]   I. Title.
TL793.D36   1990
629.4'1—dc20   90-35012
                                           CIP
                                           AC

Dillon Press, Inc., 242 Portland Avenue South Minneapolis, Minnesota 55415

Printed in the United States of America
1 2 3 4 5 6 7 8 9 10 99 98 97 96 95 94 93 92 91 90

Photographic Acknowledgments
The photographs are reproduced through the courtesy of the California Institute of Technology; the Cerro-Tololo Inter-American Observatory; the Jet Propulsion Laboratory, California Institute of Technology; Kalmbach Publishing Co., *Astronomy* and *Odyssey* magazines; the National Aeronautics and Space Administration; Pictorial Parade, Inc./Fotos International; Seichi Kiyohara/Hughes Research Laboratories; and Gary Young/Vela Productions.

METRIC CONVERSION CHART To Find Approximate Equivalents		
WHEN YOU KNOW:	**MULTIPLY BY:**	**TO FIND:**
TEMPERATURE degrees Fahrenheit (minus 32)	0.56	degrees Celsius
LENGTH		
feet	30.48	centimeters
yards	0.91	meters
miles	1.61	kilometers
MASS (weight)		
pounds	0.45	kilograms
tons	0.91	metric tons
VOLUME		
cubic yards	0.77	cubic meters
AREA		
acres	0.41	hectares
square miles	2.59	square kilometers
CAPACITY		
gallons	3.79	liters

14.95

Contents

910098

The Challenge

"Go to warp factor five, helmsman." "Aye, aye, captain."

And with the mere flick of a switch, it is done. Leaving a dazzling trail of rainbow colors, the starship *Enterprise* flashes out of sight on its way to yet another adventure among the **stars**.* It all seems so easy. But will star travel ever be that easy and quick? Will it ever prove even possible at all?

Gaze up at the night sky, and there is nothing but a thin layer of air between you and the stars—nothing, that is, except for countless miles of empty space. Even the nearest star to Earth, beyond the Sun, lies at the fantastic distance of 25 **trillion** miles!

No one can imagine a distance that huge. But if we make a tiny scale model of everything in space, we can begin to appreciate how far away the stars are compared to our neighboring **planets**.

Suppose the Sun has been

▎Inside the starship *Enterprise.*

shrunk down to the size of a pinhead and placed in the middle of San Francisco. Then Earth would be a speck, too small to be seen, just 4 inches away. The most remote planet in the **Solar System**, Pluto, would orbit, or move around, the Sun at a distance of a little more than 12 feet. But on the same scale, the nearest star would lie beyond the city limits, 19 miles away! And that is only the nearest star. Some of the stars you can see in the night sky would be as far off as Detroit—more than 2,000 miles dis-

*Words in **bold type** are explained in the glossary at the end of this book.

tant—while others would be in London, Sydney, and Moscow.

Speed and Distance

So, could you ever fly to the stars? That depends on whether we can ever build spacecraft that can cover trillions of miles in much less than a human lifetime.

Interstellar distances—the gaps between stars—are so great that astronomers don't usually measure them in miles or kilometers. Instead, they use **light-years**. One light-year is the distance that light, speeding along at 186,282 miles per second, travels in a year. It equals slightly less than 6 trillion miles. By this reckoning, the nearest star is 4.2 light-years away.

But light is the fastest thing in the Universe. Even our swiftest spaceships today seem barely to move by comparison.

To break free of Earth's pull of **gravity**, a spacecraft has to gain a cruising speed of about 25,000 miles per hour. If it then maintained that speed, it could reach the planet Mars in about three months. A trip to Jupiter would last two years, while a direct flight to Pluto would take 10 times as long. Still, the planets that go around our own sun are much closer to us than any other star. At a steady 25,000 miles per hour, the trip to Proxima Centauri—the nearest star to Earth beyond the Sun—would take 114,000 years!

Even if we could somehow make our present-day spacecraft a thousand times faster, they still could not reach any other star within an average person's lifetime. Does that mean star travel will forever remain a dream? Does it mean that a real starship *Enterprise* is impossible to build? Certainly, there are difficult scientific problems that must first be solved. But scientists already know of several ways in theory to make superfast spaceships. Some of these new types of spacecraft could approach the speed of light itself. And there may even be a way of breaking through the light barrier.

Later, we shall explore some of these exciting ideas for possible future starships. But first, we will see how far we have already progressed along the road to the stars.

The launch of the space shuttle. The shuttle has three parts—a 154-foot fuel tank, two solid rocket boosters, and an orbiter that takes astronauts and cargo into space.

Rrrocket!

ushing a brilliant geyser of flame, the space shuttle orbiter *Discovery* soars into the blue of a still Florida sky. The date is September 29, 1988. American astronauts are back in space again after the disastrous explosion of the shuttle *Challenger* more than two years earlier.

It seems incredible, watching the shuttle in action, that the Space Age began as recently as 1957. On October 4 of that year, people around the world listened in amazement to the steady "beep-beep-beep" of radio signals from *Sputnik 1*. This Soviet space probe was the first human-made object to be launched into orbit around the Earth.

Since that historic day, the race into space has been rapid and dramatic. In 1961, the first human space traveler, Yuri Gargarin, blasted off from a launch pad in the Soviet Union. Just eight years later, Neil Armstrong and Edwin Aldrin stepped out of their lunar module onto the barren, dusty surface of the Moon.

Meanwhile, robot space probes ventured much further afield. They flew by or landed on Venus, Mercury, and Mars. Others flashed past the distant, giant worlds of Jupiter and Saturn. They plunged into the dusty tail of Halley's Comet. And, in 1986, one of these spacecraft photographed clearly for the first time the mysterious planet Uranus and its weird collection of moons.

Those sensational pictures of Uranus, and similar ones of Neptune in 1989, were taken by the most successful robot probe so far— *Voyager 2*. Now, like its sister craft, *Voyager 1*, and the smaller *Pioneer 10* and *11*, it is leaving our solar system forever, bound for the stars.

We shall never know what happens to *Voyager 2* or our three other primitive "star probes." By 2020, all of their batteries will be dead, and they will have

Voyager 2 took this picture of Neptune's large moon, Triton, during its flyby of the distant planet on August 25, 1989.

no power left to send messages back to Earth. They will just float on endlessly, silently, moving ever farther from the Sun.

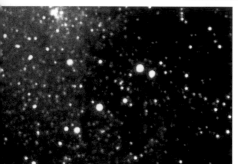

Mission specialists at the National Aeronautics and Space Administration (NASA) have calculated the paths of these spacecraft for tens of thousands of years into the future. But it seems that neither of the twin Voyagers nor the Pioneers will come closer than about one-half light-year to another star in all that time. Even if they did, people on our own planet would probably have long since forgotten or stopped caring about them.

One of the problems in traveling to the stars is that today's spacecraft are really quite slow. They may be fine for exploring the planets of our own solar system. But for interstellar journeys, they are hopelessly ill-equipped. Why should that be? Why is it that, at present, we cannot boost a spaceship to much higher speeds?

Fire and Flame
To launch a **payload** into space requires an engine

Voyager 2:
Space Probe Bound for the Stars

Once every 175 years, the giant outer planets—Jupiter, Saturn, Uranus, and Neptune—line up in a special way that allows a spacecraft to visit them all. Each planet's gravity speeds up the spacecraft and bends its flight path toward the next world. The last time this happened was in the late 1970s. *Voyager 2*, launched on August 20, 1977, was able to take full advantage of it.

Having flown by Jupiter, Saturn, and Uranus, *Voyager 2* completed its remarkable mission by skimming past the surface of Neptune on August 25, 1989. For many more years, Voyager will continue to send back information about interplanetary space. It may even help us to locate the boundary where the Solar System ends and true interstellar space begins.

Sometime between the years 2010 and 2020, Voyager's nuclear power source will run out. Although we shall lose touch with it then, mission specialists have worked out what might happen to the probe in the future. According to their calculations, *Voyager 2* will eventually come within about half a light-year of the brightest star in our sky, Sirius. Just in case any intelligent Sirians are watching, the spacecraft carries a phonograph disk with various sights and sounds of Earth recorded on it. Don't wait on the edge of your seat, though, for an alien reply. Voyager's flyby of Sirius will not happen until the year 359,900!

that can do two main things. First, it must be able to push the payload—a spacecraft and its contents—high enough and fast enough that it does not fall back to Earth. Second, it must be able to work outside the atmosphere.

If you have ever shinnied up a rope, you know how hard it is to oppose the Earth's gravitational pull. Every second you climb, you have to use a great deal of energy to fight the constant downward tug of gravity. Even just holding on takes a lot

of effort because you have to support your own **weight**. And if you want to reach the top before your energy runs out, you have to climb quickly using a force that is much larger than your weight.

Now imagine the effort needed to lift a 100-ton spacecraft (the take-off weight of the shuttle's orbiter) more than 115 miles above the ground! Yet the idea is the same. The spacecraft has to gain speed and height quickly enough to overcome the downward pull of gravity before its fuel runs out.

The only way it can do this is by rapidly burning an energy-rich fuel in a rocket engine. That creates an upward **thrust**, or pushing force, much greater than the spacecraft's weight.

There are other possible types of rockets that give a gentler thrust over a much longer period of time. These would work well in space. But they would be useless for blasting a spacecraft away from a planet's surface. To climb into orbit, or to break free of Earth's gravity altogether, requires an engine that provides a brief but very powerful lift.

Wouldn't jet engines work? They can lift a plane as big as a jumbo jet 40,000 feet off the ground. But a jet can operate only where there is air. The jet uses oxygen in the air to burn fuel, which pro vides the plane with forward thrust. Rockets, on the other hand, do not need oxygen from outside. They carry their own supply with them, either as liquid oxygen or as oxygen particles mixed with solid fuel. As a result, they can work both in the atmosphere and in space.

Take the shuttle again as an example. The

spacecraft's main engines burn a mixture of liquid oxygen and liquid **hydrogen** stored separately in a large tank. In addition, twin solid rocket boosters (SRBs) provide a massive extra thrust for the first two minutes after launch. At a height of about 28 miles, the SRBs drop away on parachutes, while the shuttle's three main engines continue firing. Six minutes later, having lifted the spacecraft to a height of about 115 miles and a speed of 17,600 miles per hour, the main engines also stop burning fuel. Now the shuttle is in orbit.

To blast a spaceship with astronauts to the Moon or to send a robot probe to Venus, the same basic method has to be used. Because of the need to overcome Earth's gravity, only a powerful chemical rocket will provide enough thrust. But why can't such a rocket propel a spacecraft at much higher speed toward the stars?

A Vital Formula

More than 300 years ago, the famous English scientist, Isaac Newton, wrote down three basic laws describing how things move. One of these, Newton's third law, says that "action and reaction are equal

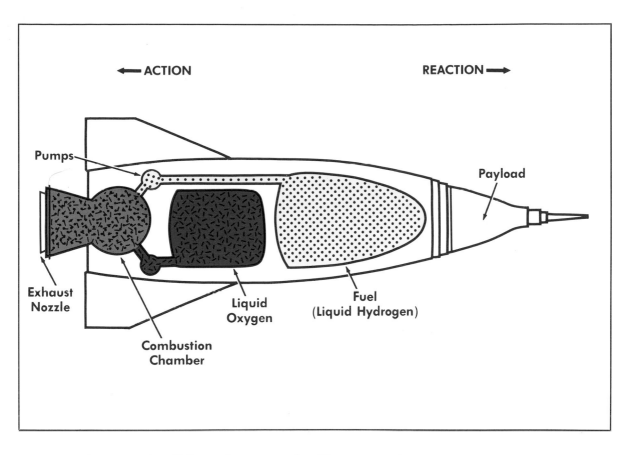

ACTION ←

REACTION →

Pumps

Payload

Exhaust
Nozzle

Liquid
Oxygen

Fuel
(Liquid Hydrogen)

Combustion
Chamber

and opposite." In other words, if you push on some-thing, it will push back on you just as hard.

Imagine how this discovery of Newton's applies to a rocket. When rocket fuel burns, it turns into a hot gas that rushes out in all directions. The tiny particles of gas press hard against the walls of the **combustion chamber** in which the fuel is burned. At the rear of the combustion chamber is an opening. Many speeding gas particles escape in this direction through an **exhaust** nozzle without pushing against anything. But those that hit the front of the chamber do push. Since this push is the only one not bal-anced by an equal and opposite force, it causes the spacecraft to move forward.

This diagram shows the basic parts of a rocket.

Rocket engines such as those used on the shuttle give an enormous forward shove to the spacecraft. Together, the shuttle's main engines and twin SRBs develop nearly 7 million pounds of thrust at take-off. The astronauts are pressed back in their seats with a force equal to that of three Earth gravities. For several minutes, the shuttle gains speed at the astonishing rate of more than 40 miles per hour every second! But to accelerate that hard also means that each second thousands of gallons of fuel have to be burned. Within a short time the shuttle reaches orbit, but its main fuel supplies have been completely used up.

Now imagine that we wanted to use chemical rockets, not to launch the space shuttle, but to power a starship. To save fuel and effort, suppose that we assemble this spacecraft in orbit from pieces carried up by the shuttle. Also, we will arrange to burn fuel on the starship much more slowly. As a result, the thrust will be gentler, but it will also go on for much longer. In this way, we hope, the starship will eventually reach a tremendously high speed so that it can travel to the nearest star within 10 or 20 years.

Work begins. We order the largest rocket engines ever made, huge fuel tanks, and millions of gallons of fuel to last during the journey there and back. But then the chief engineer points out that our plan will not work. The highest speed that exhaust gases can escape from a chemical rocket, he says, is about 2.5 miles per second. That limits how fast the spacecraft can go, he explains. There is a formula that links four important quantities: the **exhaust speed** of the gases from the rocket, the spacecraft's

The Saturn V main engine, used to launch the Apollo spacecraft to the Moon, was the most powerful rocket engine ever made.

17

final speed, its starting **mass**, and its final mass. Mass measures how hard it is to make an object move or change its speed.

"Sounds complicated," we say. "Get to the bottom line, chief."

"It's like this," he goes on. "If you want this starship to reach a final speed of 10 miles a second, it has to start out with 55 times more mass than it ends up with. Most of that starting mass is fuel."

Ten miles a second! Is the chief kidding? That is not much faster than *Voyager 2*. It would still take 80,000 years to reach Proxima Centauri at that rate!

"We need 50,000 miles per second final speed, chief. Anything less, and the astronauts would never live to see Earth again."

"No way," he replies. "To reach even 20 miles a second with these conventional engines, you would need fuel with a mass of more than 3,000 times the rest of the ship put together. To get up to 40 miles a second, you would have to have a fuel mass of 9 million times that of the payload! It all goes back to the low exhaust speed of a chemical rocket. The

18

only way you are ever going to build a fast starship is to come up with a totally new type of engine. That engine would shoot out an exhaust at a much higher speed than any chemical rocket can. And it would do it with a reasonable thrust over a period of months or even years."

So there lies the difficulty with today's rockets. They fire out gases at a fairly low speed. Because of this, the spacecraft has to start out with a very high mass—mostly fuel—in order to reach a speed of even 30,000 or 40,000 miles per hour. To go even faster, so much fuel is needed that it becomes hopelessly impractical. Very high speed spacecraft will have to be powered by engines that shoot out a very high speed exhaust while still developing a reasonable thrust. Only then can the starting mass of such a spacecraft be kept down to a manageable level.

But how can we achieve that high-speed exhaust? What kind of engine can drive a spaceship to the stars?

In this artist's view, the starship *Daedalus* is assembled in Earth orbit from parts carried into space by shuttle-type craft.

Interstellar Overdrive

T he year is 2090. From its fueling base near the giant planet Jupiter, a remarkable spacecraft is setting out on the first mission ever attempted to another star. It is the robot probe *Daedalus*, and its target is Barnard's Star. This is a small, dim star, 5.9 light-years away, that may have planets circling around it.

Daedalus's journey will take only 50 years at a top speed of 22,000 miles per second, or one-eighth the speed of light. To go that fast, the spacecraft will rely on a totally new method of propulsion. Each second, 250 small nuclear explosions, like miniature hydrogen bombs, will be set off in the starship's engine chamber.

The hot gas produced by these explosions will be focused by a powerful force of magnetism into an exhaust jet that streams out behind the spacecraft. The speed of the escaping gases will be around 6,250 miles per second—2,500 times faster than the exhaust of an ordinary chemical rocket. The fast-moving jet of gas will drive the 54,000-ton *Daedalus* forward with a thrust of 1.7 million pounds.

For more than two years, the big, first-stage engines of *Daedalus* will fire, accelerating the probe to a speed of 13,200 miles per second. Then the empty fuel tanks and motors of the first stage will be released into space, and the second-stage engines will be started. Exactly three years and 290 days into the mission, these smaller engines, too, will stop firing. The spacecraft will have reached its final cruising speed, ready for a 47-year coast to Barnard's Star.

All this may seem to be just another fantastic idea from science fiction, like the starships in the movies and on television. But, in fact, it is more than that. *Daedalus* may not have been built yet;

perhaps it never will be. But a detailed design for it does exist, and there is no reason why a spacecraft like it could not be launched sometime in the next century.

Blueprint for a Starship

The idea for *Daedalus* comes from a team of scientists and engineers whose efforts were coordinated by the British Interplanetary Society. Their goal was to see if a spacecraft, capable of reaching a nearby star in 50 years or less, could be designed and built in the near future.

The main problem was to decide what kind of **propulsion system**—the system used to push the spacecraft forward—to use. In the end, the design team settled for a system that worked by nuclear fusion. This is the same process by which the Sun makes its heat and light.

In nuclear fusion, particles of a lighter substance, such as hydrogen, are slammed together at very high temperatures to form particles of a heavier substance, such as **helium**. In the process, a tiny bit of mass is lost. That mass is turned into a huge

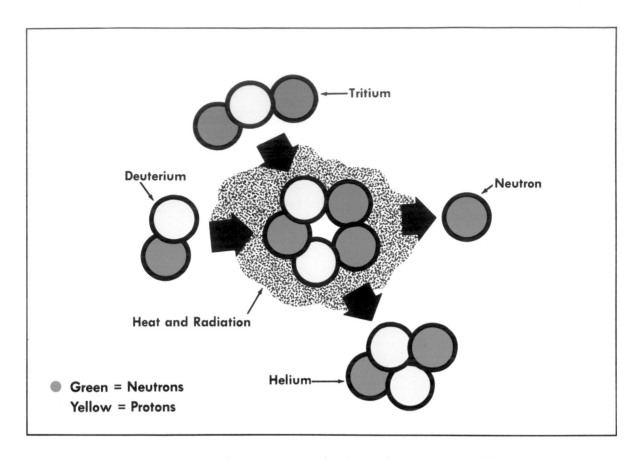

Tritium

Deuterium

Neutron

Heat and Radiation

Helium

● Green = Neutrons
Yellow = Protons

In this fusion reaction, two types of hydrogen, deuterium and tritium, combine to form helium nuclei. In the process, tiny particles called neutrons are released.

amount of energy, including the energy of motion of the particles created in the reaction. Since these fast-moving particles also carry an electric charge, they can be guided and focused by a **magnetic field**. This would be an ideal means, the *Daedalus* scientists reasoned, to drive their spacecraft to the stars.

Little pellets of fusion fuel would be shot into the engine chamber at the back of the spacecraft at the rate of 250 a second. Each would be met by a short, but incredibly powerful burst of particles called **electrons**. This burst would trigger the fusion reaction. In an instant the pellet would explode with the force of several tons of TNT, a high explosive. Most of the hot, charged gas from the explosion

24

would be channeled into an exhaust jet to push the spacecraft forward. A small fraction of the gas would be used to supply the energy for the next electron burst.

When it reached Barnard's Star, *Daedalus* would start its busy observation program. Small scoutships would head out from the main spacecraft to explore the surface of any newfound worlds. By means of a powerful on-board computer, *Daedalus* would examine all of the incoming data and radio back the most important findings to Earth.

But the one thing *Daedalus* could not do, once it had arrived at its destination, is stop! Within a few days of its encounter, the spacecraft would be heading away from Barnard's Star, still moving at one-eighth the speed of light.

Human Missions to the Stars

Why couldn't *Daedalus* be brought to a halt as it neared its target? The superfast spacecraft could not stop because to lose speed is just as hard as to gain it. For *Daedalus* to brake from one-eighth light-speed would take as much fuel as to accelerate to that speed. If fuel for braking were taken along, then

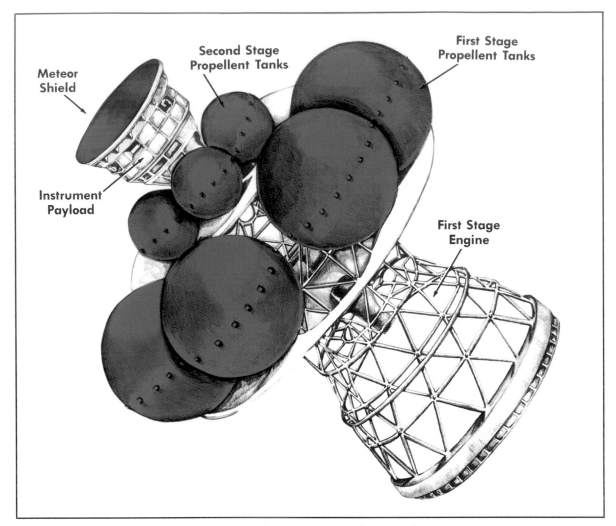

Meteor
Shield

Second Stage
Propellent Tanks

First Stage
Propellent Tanks

Instrument
Payload

First Stage
Engine

this would greatly increase the probe's starting mass. As a result, much more fuel would be needed to propel the spacecraft to its cruising speed.

The figures work out like this. Simply to fly by Barnard's Star, without slowing down, *Daedalus* would have to begin its mission with 46,000 tons of fuel. But in order for it to stop when it reached the star, it would need to start with 46,000 times 46,000, or more than 2 **billion** tons! Carrying that much fuel would pose a tremendous engineering

Sailing on a Wind of Light

Hold your hand in front of a flashlight, and the light from it causes a very slight pressure against your hand. Although you cannot possibly feel it, because the pressure is so small, light does push. This has led to an interesting idea for a robot spacecraft.

Imagine that, orbiting around the Sun, is a fantastically strong source of light. It is a **laser**, a device for producing light in intense, pure, narrow beams. This particular laser is billions of times more powerful than any in use today.

Stopped some distance in front of the laser is a very unusual spaceship. The main part of it consists of a round sail of aluminum, 62 miles across but less than a millionth of an inch thick! Attached to the center of this fine, metallic sail is the spacecraft's scientific and communications equipment. There are no fuel tanks or rocket engines, because they are not needed. This is a spaceship made to catch a wind of light.

Suddenly, the laser bursts into life. Its powerful rays, trained accurately on the giant sail, begin to push the strange spacecraft away. Steadily, the spacecraft begins to gather speed. After 18 months of being pushed by the laser beam, it is moving at half the speed of light. Now the laser is turned off, allowing the ship to coast toward its destination—one of the stars nearest to the Sun.

This remarkable idea is not without its problems. For instance, it would be extremely difficult to keep a laser beam tightly focused on the probe's light-sail over great distances. Also, tiny particles of dust in space would tend to scatter and weaken the laser light. Finally, if the star probe could reach very high speeds,

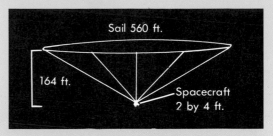

The "Sunflower" sailing craft has an aluminized "sail" made of 480 individual petals. The spacecraft itself consists of a two-by-four-foot cylinder, tethered to the sail by wires and a boom.

its slender sail would be in danger of being wrecked by dust particles as it collided with them.

Another idea for sailing on a wind of light, called "photosailing," is a spaceship powered by the flow of photons, or particles of light, from the Sun. Scientists from NASA's Jet Propulsion Laboratory formed the World Space Foundation to help plan and design this kind of solar-powered spacecraft. By 1990, scientists from six nations had designed "sailing ships" for a race from Earth to Mars. Called the Columbus 500 Space Sail Cup, the race has been timed to take place on the 500th anniversary of Columbus's discovery of the Americas.

If all goes as planned, the spacecraft will be launched on normal rockets and sent into orbit near the starting line, within 1,000 miles of Earth. Then the craft, which are quite small with their sails folded, will unfurl very thin plastic and aluminum sails and catch the Sun's light. For months they will gain speed slowly because they are "sailing" against the strong pull of the Earth's gravity. Eventually they could reach a speed of 60,000 miles per hour, and arrive at Mars in about 250 days. The first designs for the U.S. craft have been completed, but backers of the project must raise enough money to build and launch the U.S. entry in time for the planned 1992 race.

problem for the spacecraft's designers.

Yet, if people are ever to travel to the stars, they will want to stop when they arrive. And unless they intend to stay forever, they will need some means to get back home. It might be possible, for instance, to build a much larger version of the *Daedalus* probe that would carry a human crew. This starship would have enough fuel on board to slow it down at its destination. Then the crew would refill their fuel tanks for the return journey to Earth, using material obtained from the planetary system they were exploring. Such a mission would still involve billions of tons of fuel that would have to be carried on the journeys both to and from the star. There would also be a risk of the astronauts becoming stranded if they failed to find enough fuel halfway through the mission.

Scientists, however, have proposed a different way to power a starship with a human crew. According to this plan, not only can we avoid carrying huge amounts of fuel aboard a starship, we can avoid carrying any fuel at all!

28

Have Scoop, Will Travel

The great gaps between stars are, in fact, not completely empty. Spread very thinly throughout interstellar space are particles of hydrogen. If a spacecraft could somehow collect enough of this hydrogen as it moved along, it could use these particles as a fusion fuel to propel it to the stars.

Because some of the hydrogen in space carries an electrical charge, it could be dragged into the spacecraft by a powerful magnetic field. That field could be generated by an enormous, funnel-shaped scoop, made of wire mesh, attached to the front of the ship. After being sucked in, as if by a huge vacuum cleaner, the particles of hydrogen would be fused together to produce a hot, fast exhaust. In this way the starship, called an **interstellar ram-jet**, would be driven forward.

The faster the ram-jet traveled, the more hydrogen it would "ram" into, and so the more fuel it would have to increase its speed. Eventually, this kind of starship would come very close to the speed of light itself.

29

But what about slowing down? Again, the ram-jet has a big advantage over other types of space-craft. Simply by reversing its magnetic field, the star-ship could push away the hydrogen in front of it. This would have the effect of gradually cutting the ram-jet's speed until it arrived at its destination far-away in space.

Some quite difficult problems will have to be overcome, though, before an interstellar ram-jet can be built. First, a ram-jet engine could not work

effectively at low speeds. A second type of engine, then, such as the one proposed for the *Daedalus* probe, would be needed to make the starship reach a speed at which the ram-jet could take over. Since this engine would add greatly to the ship's mass, it would make the probe harder to accelerate.

A more serious problem is posed by dust particles in space. Although they are tiny and widely scattered, these particles would cause severe damage if they smashed into the starship at tens of thousands of miles per second. The damage would be even greater because the mass of objects increases with increasing speed. From the point of view aboard the starship, the dust would be rushing toward it very quickly. As a result, each dust particle would appear to have the mass of a large boulder. A powerful shield of some kind would be needed to deflect the dust before it slammed into the main body of the spacecraft.

Let us assume, though, that problems such as these can eventually be solved. Imagine that, in time, an interstellar ram-jet is built that can travel almost at the speed of light. It would certainly work for taking human crews back and forth between the Sun and the nearest stars. A round trip to Proxima Centauri, for instance, would take less than 10 years.

But most stars in space are much farther away than Proxima Centauri. To go on a round-trip journey to a star that is 50 light-years away, even at the speed of light, would take 100 years. What is more.

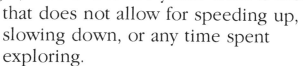

that does not allow for speeding up, slowing down, or any time spent exploring.

One idea that was first suggested many years ago is a "space ark." This would be a starship big enough for hundreds or even thousands of men, women, and children to travel in. During its voyage to a distant star, several generations of people aboard might be born, live out their lives, and die. Those who were adults when the ship reached its destination could be the great-great grandchildren of those who set out from Earth. But even though a space ark could be built in the future, it might be very hard to find volunteers for the crew!

In fact, there is a much easier way for people to reach distant stars without growing old and dying before they arrive. This has to do with the strange things that happen close to the speed of light.

On board starships that travel close to the speed of light, time, mass, and length are not the same as on Earth. Here, a shuttle craft leaves the mother ship to land on a new world faraway in space.

Through the Light Barrier

The fastest that most people ever travel on Earth is about 600 miles per hour, the cruising speed of a jumbo jet. Compare this with the 670 million miles per hour of a light ray, and it is clear that we have no experience of really high speeds at all.

Still, we can use our common sense. The only effect of traveling very fast would be to make the time of our journey shorter. Whether we travel at 5 miles per hour or at 500 million miles per hour should not make any difference apart from getting us to our destination much quicker. Isn't that right?

No—it is wrong. In 1905, the brilliant German scientist Albert

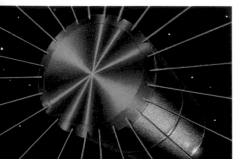

Einstein caused a revolution in the way we think about the Universe. In his special **theory of relativity**, he showed that quantities such as mass, length, and time are not as fixed as they seem. In fact, very odd things start to happen when objects move relative to one another at speeds close to that of light.

The Curious Case of the Mixed-Up Clocks

Suppose a spaceship makes a round trip to the nearest star, Proxima Centauri, at a steady nine-tenths of the speed of light. (We will assume that it comes straight back without stopping.) Then to everyone on Earth, the journey will seem to have taken about 9.5 years. Yet, according to clocks carried aboard the spacecraft, only slightly more than 4 years will have gone by. Incredibly, the astronauts will have aged 5.5 years less than their friends who stayed behind on Earth!

Strangely, as Einstein discovered, time slows down for objects traveling at extremely high speeds. If someone on Earth with a powerful telescope could watch the clocks aboard a fast-moving starship,

36

those clocks would seem to lose time. The faster the
spacecraft went, the slower the clocks would seem
to tick. Even the astronauts would appear to do everything in slow motion. Yet, from the astronauts own
point of view, aboard the starship, all would appear
normal.

Other odd changes take place, too, at high
speeds. As viewed from Earth, a fast-moving spaceship would seem to shrink along its direction of
motion. Also, its mass would increase. At nine-tenths
the speed of light, a spacecraft would look less than
half as long as it did at rest and twice as massive. Yet
to the crew, the ship would appear unchanged. To
them, dust particles and everything else in space

Albert Einstein's
theories have an
important bearing
on future missions
to the stars.

would appear more squashed together and more massive.

The changes that occur at such high speeds have an important bearing on future travel to the stars. They make it possible for astronauts to visit even very distant stars well within their own lifetimes. If the astronauts travel fast enough, they will age much more slowly than if they had stayed on Earth. For instance, a trip to a star 100 light-years away at 99 percent of the speed of light would take more than a century as measured by Earth clocks. But the astronauts who made such a journey would only age by 10 years. In starships that moved even faster, people could cross hundreds or thousands of light-years in just a few years as measured by the clocks aboard their spacecraft.

But when the crew returned from such a voyage, they would find that all their friends and relatives had long since died. The crew members would have aged by only a few years. Yet they would find that the Earth and everything on it would be centuries older than when they had left. It is hard to imagine that anyone would want to go back to a home planet they could no longer recognize.

38

On the Trail of the Starship Enterprise

In the language of *Star Trek*, "warp factor one" means the speed of light. The starship *Enterprise* crashes through the light barrier with ease. But will that ever really be possible? According to Einstein's theory of relativity, the answer is no.

Einstein calculated that as an object gathers speed, it also gains mass. The more massive something is, the harder it is to push it to still higher speeds. Eventually, a time comes when the object

On television and in the movies, the starship *Enterprise* breaks through the light barrier with a touch of the ship's controls.

39

has so much mass that it is impossible to make it go any faster. In fact, to make a spaceship reach exactly the speed of light would take more energy than there is in the whole Universe.

Einstein's theory does not mean that a starship could not go very close to the speed of light. In principle, the interstellar ram-jet could travel at 99 percent, or even 99.999 percent, of the speed of light. But it could never reach light-speed.

This limit on speed appears to mean that real starships cannot hop from star to star at warp factor one—never mind warp factor eight or nine. But

there is one other possibility that may help us break through the light barrier.

Into the Black Hole

There are some weird things in the depths of space. But perhaps the strangest of all is the **black hole**. A black hole is a place in the Universe where the pull of gravity is so strong that nothing can escape from it—not even light.

Black holes are thought to form when stars much heavier than the Sun reach the end of their lives.

When a massive star has used up all its available fuel for making new light and heat, the outer parts of it are blown away in a monstrous explosion called a supernova. The remains of the wrecked star—its burned-out core—may then shrink in the wink of an eye until it is smaller than the dot over this *i*.

Although the once-bright star has now become tiny, its gravitational pull, close by, is very strong. From within a radius of about 10 miles of the dead star, nothing can escape. This is the region of the black hole.

Scientists are not sure what black holes are like inside. They believe that if a spaceship fell into the kind of black hole that forms when a big star dies, that ship would be rapidly torn apart.

But there may be other kinds of black holes. Some of these may be much larger and more massive. The gravitational pull of a supermassive black hole would be extremely powerful. Yet, it might not prove as damaging to a spacecraft, because the difference in the pull between one end of the spacecraft and the other would be far less than in the case of a small black hole. A starship might be able to

enter such an object without being destroyed. If so, that might create a remarkable opportunity. According to some suggestions, such a black hole could be used as a way to jump instantly to other, perhaps remote places in the Universe.

At the moment it is just an idea. But black holes may be like the entrances to subway tunnels that connect many different places in space and time. The tunnels themselves are known as "wormholes." And just as a black hole could be the way into a wormhole, a "white hole" could be the way back out. In theory, a spaceship could travel along wormholes and pop up in a place tens or even millions of light-years away from where it entered. That journey could be made in a very short time. The spaceship might even appear in the far future or in the past, and then travel back to its own space and time by going back through the wormhole the other way. Traveling in this way, the speed of light would no longer be a barrier. But if such a journey through time and space is possible, it remains hundreds of years in the future.

In this artist's view, an interstellar spacecraft approaches a black hole.

A wide-angle view of the Milky Way, our galaxy, in the direction of its center.

Star Trekking

With your eyes alone, away from the glare of street lights, you can see about 2,000 stars on a clear night. Binoculars or a small telescope will show you many more. In fact, our sun belongs to a huge, spiral-shaped star city, or **galaxy**, of about 200 billion stars. What is more, astronomers estimate that there may be about 100 billion galaxies. That makes a grand total, for the whole Universe, of about 10 billion trillion stars—enough to keep even the most ambitious space explorers busy for a long time to come. But of that great mass of stars, which ones will the people of Earth choose to visit first?

In Search of Alien Worlds

Stars come in an immense variety. There are giants
and dwarfs, hot stars and cool stars, and stars alone
or with companions. Stars also differ greatly in the
amount of light they give off. In fact, the brightest
stars you can see in the sky may not be the closest.
For example, the nearest star to the Sun, Proxima

Centauri, is a very dim kind of star called
a red dwarf. You would need a powerful
telescope to be able to see it. On the
other hand, the brilliant orange star Be-
telgeuse, in the constellation, or star pat-
tern, of Orion, is more than 300 light-
years away. It is a supergiant, so large
that if it were put in place of the Sun, it would cover
the orbits of Mercury, Venus, Earth, and Mars.

Other bright stars are among our neighbors. Sirius, for example, the brightest star in the sky,
is slightly more than eight light-years away from
Earth. Although it is really much fainter than Betel-
geuse, it appears to be brighter because it is so
much closer to us. Alpha Centauri, another brilliant
star, can be seen only from the Southern Hemi-
sphere. It belongs to the same star system as Proxi-

ma Centauri, and lies at roughly the same distance.

The first stars to be visited, either by robot probes or astronauts aboard starships, will be the ones that are fairly nearby. But even within 20 light-years of the Sun, there is quite a selection of stars to choose from. A number of red dwarfs, one or two Sun-like stars, and Sirius are among the possible choices.

Decisions about future missions to the stars may be based on whether or not a star has planets. In addition to providing a place for a space-craft to land, some planets of other stars may support alien forms of life. At the very least, there may be worlds that would be suitable for human beings to colonize or explore.

Today, even the largest telescope on Earth cannot show planets orbiting around other stars. The best evidence we have comes from the wobbles produced by the gravitational pull of extremely massive planets on their parent stars. Such wobbles may have been detected in the movement of Barnard's Star. That discovery helped convince the *Daedalus* design team to

A Travel Guide to Nearby Stars

Pretend you are in charge of planning the first human mission to another star. Look at the following brief reports about some of the nearest stars and decide what you think might be the best target.

Star: Alpha Centauri
Distance: 4.3 light-years. Actually, a three-star system made up of two bright stars, Alpha Centauri A and B, that are close together, and a dim, red dwarf, Proxima Centauri, that orbits around this pair. The nearest star system to the Sun. No known planets.

Star: Barnard's Star
Distance: 5.9 light-years. A small red dwarf about 2,000 times dimmer than the Sun. Thought to have at least two large planets circling around it.

Star: Lalande 211385
Distance: 8.2 light-years. Another red dwarf but larger and brighter than Barnard's Star. Thought to have at least one planet.

Star: Sirius
Distance: 8.7 light-years. The brightest star as seen from Earth, 26 times brighter than the Sun and about 20 times as big. May possibly have planets. Also has an interesting companion star, Sirius B, orbiting around it. Sirius B, an object known as a white dwarf, is the squashed remains of a dead star.

Star: Epsilon Eridani
Distance: 10.8 light-years. The nearest star that is both reasonably like the Sun (though only about one-third as bright) and alone. If it has any planets, there is a chance that they may support life.

Star: Sigma Pavonis
Distance: 20 light-years. An almost exact copy of the Sun—very similar in size, color, and brightness. If there is a planet in orbit around this star at about the same distance as Earth from the Sun, it might be an ideal place for humans to colonize.

suggest it as a target for their robot probe.

Future space travelers may also choose to visit a star that closely resembles the Sun. A planet circling such a star at about the distance of Earth from the Sun might be an ideal place for humans to land on and build colonies. Nearby, Sun-like stars include Alpha Centauri (4.3 light-years away), Epsilon

At the Challenger Center in Houston, Texas, young people go on an imaginary space mission.

Eridani (10.8 light-years away), and Tau Ceti (11.6 light-years away).

Why Fly to the Stars?

However it is achieved, crossing trillions and trillions of miles of space to reach other stars will involve a huge effort. It will be risky, time-consuming, and expensive. So, why should we bother?

Wouldn't it make more sense to stay here on Earth where conditions are just right for us, and we have everything we need?

Many arguments have been put forward in support of space travel. Mining raw materials on other worlds, relieving the world's population problem, learning more about the Universe—these are just some of the reasons people have suggested. But the most important reason of all has no practical value. It is simply that human beings like to explore.

If there is somewhere that no one has ever seen or traveled to, sooner or later men and women will choose to go there. It is the same urge that has driven explorers to face great dangers in their quest to reach the frozen poles, penetrate the steamy, tropical jungles, or climb the highest mountains. Now we are running out of new frontiers to explore on Earth. We have begun to look, first to the other worlds of our solar system, and then to the distant worlds of other stars.

No one can say when the first robot probe will leave on its journey to Barnard's Star, or Alpha Centauri, or another stellar neighbor of the Sun. But it will happen. And, in time, humans will follow and cross the vast interstellar spaces themselves.

To begin with, they may simply stop for a while to explore the strange, new worlds of other stars. But later, they will build bases and, eventually, great cities on some of those alien planets. Over many years, the human race will spread from star to star, moving ever more deeply into the uncharted reaches of the  Galaxy. We may even encounter other races of beings, perhaps more advanced than ourselves. If we can solve the difficult problems we face on our planet today, we have a tremendous future ahead of us in the great, unexplored Universe.

Could you, then, ever travel to the stars? We have seen that the answer is definitely yes. *Daedalus*-like probes could probably be constructed and launched by late in the twenty-first century. Faster, human-carrying starships, such as the interstellar ram-jet, may not be built until much later. Today, it is too early to tell if we will ever be able to hop from star to star, or from galaxy to galaxy, with the help of black hole "subways." But the fact that we can already talk about such an incredible way to travel is encouraging.

The stars challenge us every night with their beauty and mystery. Someday we shall accept that challenge.

In the future, humans will cross the vast reaches of space between the Sun and other stars. As this artist imagines, they will, in time, explore new, earthlike worlds.

Hands On

Build a rocket engine from a chicken's egg. This engine works by the same principle as the engines of future starships. Its jet of steam allows it to propel a simple boat. *You will need:*

- An uncracked raw chicken's egg
- A fine knitting needle
- A basin
- All-purpose glue
- A metal foil food container (such as TV dinners come in)
- Scissors
- A paper clip
- A few inches of stiff wire
- A candle

Wash the outside of the egg and pierce a tiny hole through it, from end to end, using the knitting needle. Hold the egg over a basin and blow through one of the holes. The yolk and white of the egg will come out of the hole at the other end of the shell and fall into the basin. Hold the eggshell under water and remove it when it is about half full. Put your fingers over the holes and shake it to clean the inside. Blow out the contents, then rinse the eggshell again in the same way. Now dry the outside of the shell and seal one of the holes with a blob of thick glue. Leave the glue to set.

54

Make the boat from the metal food container. Trim the sides with scissors and bend one end to form the boat's curved bow. Clip a small flap of scrap foil to the stern of the boat to act as a rudder. Bend the piece of wire to form a cradle for the eggshell. Cut a small piece from the top of the candle. Hold the shell under water so that a little water enters. Do not let too much in as it will take a long time to boil. Using hand-hot water will speed things up. Arrange the candle stump, wire frame, and shell as shown and light the candle with an adult's help. After a few minutes, the boat will move forward, driven by the thrust of the eggshell rocket.

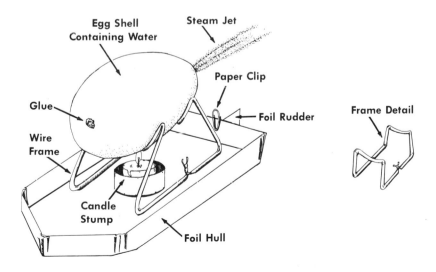

Glossary

billion—one thousand million, or 1,000,000,000

black hole—a region of space where the pull of gravity is so strong that nothing, not even light, can escape. One way that black holes are thought to form is when the cores of very massive stars fall in upon themselves

combustion chamber—the part of a rocket engine in which the fuel is burned to produce exhaust gases that drive the spacecraft forward

electron—a tiny particle, even smaller than a proton or a neutron

exhaust—the waste material produced when a fuel is burned. The reactive force arising from the exhaust as it escapes from the combustion chamber causes a spacecraft to gain speed

exhaust speed—the speed at which the exhaust material from a rocket engine leaves the spacecraft. A high exhaust speed is important if the spacecraft's final speed is also to be high

fusion—a process in which the most basic particles, or nuclei, of a lighter substance combine to make nuclei of a heavier substance. During nuclear fusion, a small amount of mass is transformed into a very large amount of energy. The most common and energy-rich fusion reaction is that in which hydrogen nuclei collide, at high temperatures, and create helium nuclei

galaxy—a very large collection of stars. Galaxies come in a variety of shapes—round, oval, spiral, and odd-shaped—and a variety of sizes. Spiral galaxies, such as the one we live in, contain huge amounts of loose gas and dust from which future stars may be made

gravity—a force exerted by any object that has mass. The Earth's gravity is the force that prevents the atmosphere, and people, from floating away into space

helium—the second lightest and most common substance in the Universe; normally found as a gas. At high temperatures, as in the center of stars, hydrogen will fuse to form helium, producing huge amounts of energy in the process

hydrogen—the lightest and most common substance in the Universe; normally found as a gas. At high temperatures, as in the center of stars, hydrogen will fuse to form helium, producing huge amounts of energy in the process

interstellar—a word meaning "between the stars"

interstellar ram-jet—a type of spaceship in which the fuel (mainly hydrogen) is gathered and compressed from the interstellar space ahead of the ship, using a powerful magnetic scoop

laser—a device used for producing concentrated, well-directed beams of very pure light. The waves of light in a laser beam are exactly in step with one another and all of the same length. The first laser, built in 1960, used a rod-shaped crystal of ruby

light-year—the distance traveled by light, moving at 186,282 miles per second, in one year. It equals 5.85 trillion miles

magnetic field—a region in which a force of magnetism acts

mass—anything that contains matter—for example, a rocket, a star, or a person—has mass. Mass gives a measure of how difficult it is to start moving an object that is still, or to change the speed of an object that is already moving

payload—the part of a spacecraft that does not include the fuel or propulsion system. In the case of a robot probe, the payload consists largely of scientific and communications equipment. In a spaceship with astronauts, though, a large part of the payload is made up of support systems and living quarters for the human crew

planet—a round object, usually at least several thousand miles across, that is in orbit around a star. Planets give off no light of their own and are much cooler than stars. The Sun has nine known planets, including the Earth. Many other stars probably have systems of planets

propulsion system—the means by which a spacecraft (or any other vehicle) is made to move

Solar System—the name given to the Sun and everything that goes around it, including the planets and their moons

star—a round, gassy object in space that normally makes its own light and heat by nuclear fusion. The only exceptions are "dead" stars, such as white dwarfs, neutron stars, and black holes, that have used up their supplies of fusion energy

theory of relativity—developed by the great German-American scientist Albert Einstein in the early part of the twentieth century. The so-called special theory of relativity shows how quantities such as mass, length, and time change when objects move at different relative speeds. In his general theory of relativity, Einstein describes a new theory of gravity

thrust—in rocketry, the forward force produced by a spacecraft's engine

trillion—one million million, or 1,000,000,000,000

weight—the downward force acting on an object due to gravity. A person's weight, for instance, would be different on the Moon than on Earth because the pull of gravity is different. That person's mass, though, would stay the same wherever he or she was in the Universe

Index